ROCKBRIDGE

ROCKBRIDGE

A PHOTOGRAPHIC ESSAY

Bruce Young &
Jennifer Law Young

FOREWORD BY WILLARD SCOTT

BUENA VISTA & CHARLOTTESVILLE
VIRGINIA

Copyright 2005 by Bruce Young and Jennifer Law Young

All rights reserved, including the right of reproduction in whole or part in any form.

Designed by Patricia Gibson

Edited by Andy Wolfe

1 3 5 7 9 10 8 6 4 2

Library of Congress Control Number: 2005926790
Rockbridge: A Photographic Essay
     p.   cm.
includes subject references and index.
     1. Rockbridge County, Virginia.   2. Photography.
     I. Young, Bruce K.   II. Young, Jennifer Law   III. Scott, Willard

ISBN 0-9768238-4-5 (hardcover : alk. paper)

Mariner Publishing
is a division of
Mariner Companies, Inc.
212 East 21st Street, Buena Vista, VA 24416-2716
http://www.marinermedia.com
The pen and compass rose are the trademark of Mariner Companies, Inc.

This book is printed on acid-free paper meeting the requirements of the American Standard for Permanence of Paper for Printed Library Materials
Printed in China

For our parents —

Who gave us our first cameras
&
Who taught us to appreciate the world around us.

When we decided to move our base of operations, our home, from Washington, DC, to Lexington—in Rockbridge County, Virginia—most of the people we knew thought we were positively, certifiably crazy. They had not seen what we had seen. We'd spent years covering Washington—rushing up Capitol Hill and chasing the president as part of the press pool at the White House. We'd traveled to all corners of the world creating documentaries and attempting to capture that "1,000-word photograph." What we wanted was a home that offered lots of tranquility, a sense of antiquity, quiet culture, and textured scenery. Looking back on the college years Bruce spent at Lexington's Washington & Lee University gave us a pretty good idea of where to head.

And so the story goes: We went out to purchase a "picture book" of Lexington to send to friends and family, and discovered there wasn't one in print. Right there and then we decided to make one. We started this project in 1998. After seven years and almost 5,000 images we realized we were giving new meaning to the phrase "get the picture." There are so many wonderful Rockbridge people who let us roam their property and stand on their porches to capture these images. We gratefully thank them all.

When you work for major news agencies, as we do, someone else worries about the actual publishing of your work. And, Rockbridge being the magical place that it is, we were delighted to discover a publishing company in our own backyard— with the right technology, international assets, talent and creative temperament to produce our book. Pat Gibson, Andy Wolfe, and Rick Britton worked with us, side-by-side, hour by painstaking hour, to make this book, our photographic essay, which we now humbly present to you.

Page through and see why we're *so* happy Rockbridge is our home.

Bruce and Jennifer
Lexington, Virginia
2005

FOREWORD

There is a feeling I get when I watch the sun come up over these hills and break into the valley with the fog below. It speaks to me. Looking northeast from my porch, I can see all the way to Afton Mountain and I don't see anything except what nature made. It really is a beautiful view... no civilization in a vista that is twenty miles across. I hope, for future generations, that it will stay that way.

My love affair with Rockbridge is a simple story. When I was twelve years old I traveled down to Blacksburg, Virginia, from Alexandria where I was raised. We traveled up the Shenandoah Valley—long before there was a highway—through all of the little towns. I remembered this area, from that early age, how beautiful it was, and I thought that if I could ever have a little farm someday I'd like it to be here.

Fifty years later and after a two year search, I found my farm. We drove up and down this "Burma" road and I thought this is kind of weird looking country... wild and almost like northern Scotland. All of a sudden it opened into this little valley and I said, "This is it!" We had a chicken dinner sitting on the hill looking down on that view and drew up the papers. That was ten years ago.

I've been all over Rockbridge. I love going down to Goshen, to me it's the most beautiful single spot in the country all seasons of the year. I think Lexington has a charm, almost unlike any other place I have ever visited. The atmosphere, the culture, the arts—I think you'd be hard pressed to find any spot in the world that has as much to offer. Of course the history helps my romance with this countryside.

As you turn the pages of this book... this exceptional photographic essay of the area I love so much... think of all we have and be grateful. I believe we've got it made—the best of all worlds—physically, geographically, historically and traditionally.

Willard Scott
Rat Barn Farm
2005

Cultivators of the Earth are the most virtuous
and independent citizens.

Thomas Jefferson

The secret of happiness lies in taking a genuine interest in all the details of daily life, and elevating them to art.

William Morris

The loveliest spot in Virginia!

Matthew Fontaine Maury

In all things of nature there is something of the marvelous.
Aristotle

Great things are done when men and mountains meet.

William Blake

This is a fine town [with] many fine people.
Rutherford B. Hayes

Learning is not attained by chance. It must be sought for with ardor and attended to with diligence.

Abigail Adams

The Institute gave me not only a standard of my daily conduct among men, but it endowed me with a heritage of honor and self-sacrifice.

George C. Marshall

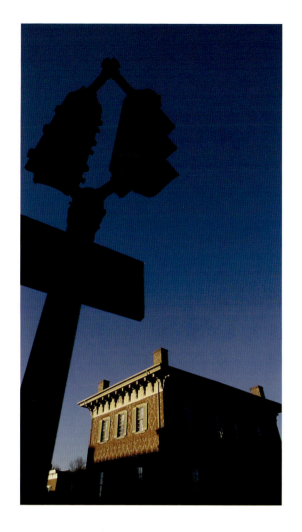

I have reported at Lexington and am delighted
with my duties, the place, and the people.

Thomas "Stonewall" Jackson

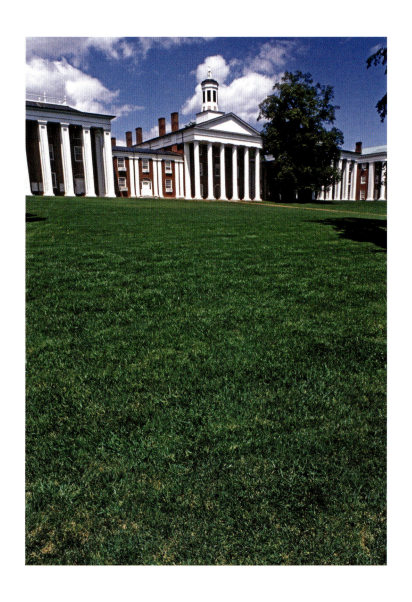

A university should be a place of light,
of liberty and of learning.

Benjamin Disraeli

To promote the Literature in this rising Empire, and to encourage the Arts, have been amongst the warmest wishes of my heart.

George Washington

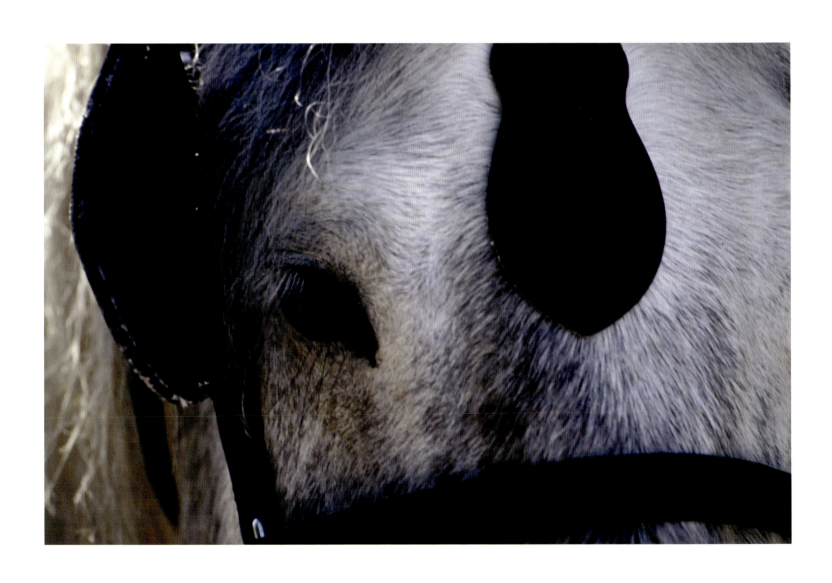

Climb the mountains and get their good tidings. Nature's peace will flow into you as sunshine flows into trees. The winds will blow their own freshness into you, and the storms their energy, while cares will drop away from you like the leaves of Autumn.

John Muir

Sometimes, if you stand on the bottom rail of a bridge and lean over to watch the river slipping slowly away beneath you, you will suddenly know everything there is to be known.

A. A. Milne

God is our only refuge and our strength.
Let us humble ourselves before Him.

Robert E. Lee

It is foolish and wrong to mourn the men who died.
Rather we should thank God that such men lived.

George S. Patton, Jr.

No occupation is so delightful to me as the culture of the earth and no culture comparable to that of the garden.

Thomas Jefferson

The Natural Bridge, the most sublime of Nature's works... so beautiful an arch, so light, and springing as it were up to heaven

Thomas Jefferson

The spirit of the valley never dies.
Lao-tzu

End Notes and Asides:

The photographs in this book are the result of solitary strolls, and family drives—we almost always go together in the car—baby in the back seat, Grammy along just for fun and a whole population wondering why the driving is so erratic. As photographers, we have very different shooting philosophies. Jennifer is target-oriented, making lists, seeking and shooting the image. Bruce, the king of weather features, is a student of the "Oh, WOW!" school of photography. Jenny is the family editor. We don't use lens filters or computer magic to enhance the images... what you see is what we saw.

Beginning at the beginning, the cover photo was a true collaborative effort. This image was our first Rockbridge Christmas card... to let friends know we had arrived. The photograph is at the Washington and Lee Colonnade. Jenny directed and Bruce took the shot at ground level.

Opening section:
Lexington by Night   This photo was taken in 2002 by Jenny. Sometimes Lexington appears urban, full of bright lights and action. This photo is a 45-second exposure with a 28 mm lens.

This next view is from the Oxford Church... It was a far away, "Oh WOW" shot for Bruce with nature providing special color and ground textures for the lens. This photo was taken with a 450 mm lens.

Dedication page:
The dedication to our parents features the Dogwood tree in their adjoining yards.

Authors' note:
Ballooning Over Town   Jenny, suffering from acrophobia, huddled in the bottom of the gondola while Bruce leaned out and got this bird's-eye view of Lexington's downtown. It was a misty morning but luckily the mist cleared as this image appeared. This 1998 photo was taken with a 20 mm lens.

Foreword:
Willard's View   On a clear day, this priceless northern Rockbridge vista stretches all the way to Afton Mountain. This is the only digital image in the book. Jenny captured the scene with a 16 mm lens.

Page 2-3
Snow Bird   This is a backyard photo that was also a Christmas card. The Cardinal appeared then disappeared then reappeared. Bruce went outside in the freezing cold and out waited the bird to capture this image with a 300 mm lens.

Page 4-5
The Horse Farm   Snow is not "usual" in Rockbridge. On this winter day, Bruce went for a solitary walk on a road off Rt. 60, west of Lexington. This image captured the cold of that afternoon with fresh snow.

Page 6
Barn Wood   This image—taken by Bruce when he got bored at an auction—is about the geometry and texture of the barn's old gate-hinge door.

Page 7
The Tractor   There it was, sitting in the field, in the cool twilight of an early summer evening: this nice old tractor. Bruce captured this bucolic image near Kerrs Creek.

Page 8
Barn Painting   As the paint fades away, this old barn near Fairfield has the look of days gone by. Rockbridge is full of old barns; we could do a book just on barns. We drove by this site hundreds of times but Jenny waited to catch this image in the snow.

Page 9
Zen and the Art of Ice   This is another backyard photo taken by Bruce. We had just come home from a trip to Russia where we made many ice images. Ice in Russia and ice in Rockbridge look exactly the same!
House Mountain   Like the bricks on the Lexington sidewalks, House Mountain is a Rockbridge icon. This particular view is a little difficult to get because the only safe place to stop is about 50 yards up the road. This book has many views of House Mountain and for the most part each is different.

Page 10
Mail Boxes   An everyday Rockbridge detail. This image was taken on a family drive. Jenny shot in one direction, Bruce shot in the other, and the baby slept in her car seat. Bruce caught this image after looking at the farm across the road. He saw the bent and bashed boxes and said, "Oh, that's neat... wild flowers, the Blue Ridge and all." We really take joy in the everyday details of life.

Page 11

The Laundry Line Driving up the road Jenny saw this image, had Bruce turn around, drive by in the other direction, turn around and drive by again. Bruce said, "Now we have to stop or that nice lady is going to worry." Jenny caught this wonderfully maternal image in the bosom of House Mountain. The lady in the yard was really very gracious; she asked if she should take down the laundry.

Page 12

Pumpkins Jenny took this shot at Dave's Produce, attracted by the shabby chic look and the very warm, rich tones.

Page 13

Autumn Leaves We don't know whose picture this is, we both shot variants of this image. We think it was taken at Washington and Lee University, but we literally have hundreds of Rockbridge foliage photos. This one was selected for its vibrant splash of varied colors.

Page 14

North to Goshen This image, taken by Bruce, was shot from Mt. Vista looking north toward Goshen. The shadow in the center looks very much like the profile of House Mountain.

Page 15

Man v. Nature This image has it all—a rich blend of natural color, the ferocity of rapids—and the solitary kayaker against it all brings it true scale. There are a thousand shades of blue in this scene caught by Bruce.

Page 16-17

The Jungle of Virginia What's around the corner is the question that comes to mind when looking at this image that Jenny captured in Irish Creek. The inner light of the photograph draws you right down the road.

Page 18-19

Visiting Our Backyard This is a photo where the subject literally came knocking at our door. We continue to be thrilled by the closeness and comfort of our natural environment. Bruce captured this image with a 300 mm lens.

Page 20

The Real Thing This image was taken from our yard. Coming from the big city, you really appreciate the sky in the valley. Skies and sunsets can be elusive and hard to catch. Bruce shot this late evening image with no filters… it's the real thing!

Page 21

Hunting on Fancy Hill Driving down US 11 we saw this hawk sitting on the fence… so we pulled over. From the car window, Bruce aimed a 300 mm lens and waited for the raptor to make his move.

Page 22

Swimming at Jordan's Point While we were making images of trees in the water, these two ducks swam up and asked to be in the picture. Jenny gave them direction for the scene she wished to capture and of course the ducks immediately swam to the appropriate position and posed.

Page 23
Flats on Cedar Creek   Jenny made this image alongside the Natural Bridge. These stair-stepping shelves are a distinctive Rockbridge feature. The colors in this image of flowing water on flat rocks provided an icing effect… nearly satin.

Page 24
The Redbud   Up on Mt. Vista, while Bruce was shooting the **North to Goshen** photo in the beginning of the book, Jenny made this image of the wonderful Redbuds and Dogwoods that populate our countryside.

Page 25
Lexington from Mt. Vista   The Blue Ridge looks small in this image taken by Bruce… it is all about the sky, and it was a beautiful shooting day. When they named this area Mt. Vista, they weren't kidding.

Page 26-27
High on the Fourth of July   On a windless morning Bruce drifted up Lexington's Main Street in a hot air balloon. This image taken with a 20 mm lens captures all of the downtown and the misty wrap of mountains. How many buildings can you identify?

Page 28-29
Lawyers Row   This wonderful 19th Century scene is one that more people really need to take the time to see. Jenny captured this image of the facades and walkway with a 16mm lens.

Page 30
Lilacs at the Green   Jenny loves Hopkins Green and looks forward to the lilacs each spring. She hopes this image, of the fence alone, clearly identifies the park and captures its spirit.

Page 31
Cornices of Lexington   While the details are different on every building—some very elaborate—they exemplify the lovely Victorian architecture throughout the cities and towns of Rockbridge. What Jenny says with this image is, "Just look up!" These are on Nelson St., photographed from Main with a 450 mm lens.

Page 32
The Shop Window   This little tableau is a display from Pumpkinseeds at Washington and Main. This image captures texture and frame. As Bruce says, "It's what happens when you let an artist run a store."

Page 32-33
Sommersby Landmark   Jenny took this image on the same day as the **Lawyers Row** photo (page 28-29) using the same 16 mm lens to look around the corner of Washington and Main. The sign is a permanent reminder of Lexington's movie-making legacy.

Page 34-35
Retreat   This image is all about sky and scale and action. Taken at the retirement parade of Sgt. Maj. Al Hockaday, a true institution at the Virginia Military Institute, it was a perfect afternoon for taking pictures. Bruce made the image with a 20 mm lens.

Page 36
September 11, 2001   The VMI cadets spontaneously draped the huge American flag on the Barracks in response to the 9/11 terrorist attacks. We shot this from every possible angle with every lens we own. We hope this image that Bruce made speaks for itself.

Page 37
Reflecting on the Barracks   Bruce planned this photo, and then he found an unwitting cadet on guard duty to fulfill the scheme. The cadet, standing at attention, provided the perfect reflection that Bruce captured with a 105 mm macro lens. The apparent speck of dust in the clouds is the American flag.

Page 38
Gothic Touch   Look up at the windows of Preston Library and you see wonderful details. Jenny loves the gothic architecture of VMI.

Page 39
The Corps Forward   Every year on May 15th, VMI remembers the cadets' valor and those who fell at the Battle of New Market, Virginia. This is a view of the parade most spectators don't get to see. Bruce captured the image inside the Stonewall Arch with a 16 mm lens.

Page 40-41
Virginia Mourning Her Dead   The trees were in full bloom. With the gothic frame of the window it was a perfect setup, but Jenny couldn't find the angle she wanted. So, a quick trip home for a ladder (for Bruce to hold) and Jenny made this very feminine image at VMI with a 300 mm lens.

Page 42
The Palms   At eight months pregnant, Jenny shot all 36 frames of this scene on a cold November night to make sure it was exactly right. Bruce once again held the ladder. Because of the long exposure time, all of the traffic lights appear green.

Page 43
Silhouettes of Lexington   The Alexander-Withrow House and the Robert E. Lee Hotel tower over the historic downtown. The angle of the canopy, along with the spires, makes Lexington look bigger than it is. Bruce used a 20 mm lens to capture these images.

Page 44
The County Courthouse   Shooting when the disposition of this building was still in question, Bruce caught this image that displays the building's gorgeous detail. The anti-pigeon spikes provide a very interesting texture and the bare tree limbs add another layer.

Page 45
Flags on Nelson Street   We believe that living in Lexington is a bit like living in a Norman Rockwell painting. Bruce captured this Americana image from the corner of Lee Ave. across from the Lexington Post Office.

Page 46-47
Misty Mountains   It's clear that Bruce really likes flying in hot-air balloons. And, after the first flight, Jenny now lets him fly alone. This photo was taken with a telephoto lens, of course, looking out across the Blue Ridge.

Page 48
Interior Inflation   Thanks to the Sunrise Rotary Club, the hot-air balloons are a real identifier of our local Fourth of July celebration. This image, shot with a 20 mm lens inside the balloon, creates an alternative view.

Page 49
Bursting in Air   For Bruce, shooting fireworks is fun and interesting, once you figure out how to do it. It's like shooting pictures of the moon; it's always daytime on the moon. So capturing fireworks is like shooting bright daylight, only with a longer exposure to capture the streaks.

Page 50-51
The Four Seasons on the Colonnade   Bruce made a similar four-season set while attending college at Washington and Lee University and recalled it was very hard to keep track of where he was standing. This series was harder, because when he made the first image—Fall—he wasn't planning on a series. The scenes were shot with a 20 mm lens, with fingers crossed in hope of being in the same place each time.

Page 52
Liberty Hall   Snow and the sunset attracted Bruce to this Rockbridge landmark… to make an image of "old" in a country that really is so new. When you are surrounded by history you can take it for granted. (At the battle of Guilford Court House, North Carolina, during the War for Independence, they could have held a meeting of the Board of Trustees of Liberty Hall Academy—they had a quorum!)

Page 53
Bearing Up   Jenny's column obsession rises again, but we are unsure of who took this shot. Its position here next to the image of the Liberty Hall ruins is a juxtaposition of what *is* against what *was*.

Page 54
Falling Snow   Living in this historic town, you have to avoid being jaded as you pass places where legends lived. Jenny has always loved these windows, and you can see the refection of the snow drifting down in this winter image of the porch at the Robert E. Lee House.

Page 55
Lee Chapel   Another day of Bruce wandering around the beautiful Washington and Lee campus. This is probably the most photographed building in Lexington. Jenny selected this image because it was a different, more pastoral composition.

Page 56-57
The General's Hand   This image of Lee Recumbent in Lee Chapel is something Jenny thought about for a long time. The detail and artistry of the sculpture, right down to the weave of the blanket, is something truly worth seeing up close.

Page 58-59
Dogwoods at the Colonnade   You can't think about Virginia or Rockbridge County without thinking about Dogwoods. Bruce took this spring image, standing in a flower bed, looking for new images of the Washington and Lee campus. One of the joys of living in this region is the four distinct seasons. Clearly that's what we were thinking about when we paired it with the fall leaves.

Page 60-61
The Wagon   On a springtime family drive, up near Mt. Vista, Bruce saw this image, stopped the car and we both jumped out and shot it. The barn wood was so full of texture and color. Bruce took this image with a 105 mm lens.

Page 62
The Fork   Jenny has a fascination with rustic objects and old wood. This image was taken at the Herb Farm near Raphine with a 28 mm lens.

Page 63
Horse Eye View   This downtown Lexington carriage horse has a timeless presence and graciously posed while Jenny got in very close with a 28 mm lens to gaze into his beautiful eyes. He made the book on looks alone.

Page 64-65
House Mountain   The icon of the county. Using a 200 mm lens, Jenny caught this vista, complete with buzzard, from a pasture near Furr's Mill Rd.

Page 66-67
The Cities   Traveling high up on the Blue Ridge Parkway, you can see the cities of Rockbridge—Buena Vista and Lexington. Jenny shot this rich mixture of sky and earth on a stormy evening, freezing in a brisk mountain breeze.

Page 68-69
Buena Vista Details   For more than a century these details—this amalgamation of architectural decoration now threatened by age and deterioration—have loomed above the entrance to the city. Everything is on this building. We really wanted to capture it before it was gone. As Jenny points out with these images, it's the original look of this town.

Page 70
The Porch   With a view over everything Buena Vista, Jenny saw this image at Southern Virginia University during a rain storm. Imagine all the history that has taken place on the boards of this Richardsonian Romanesque palace. From hotel to Southern Seminary College to the University—more than a century, and it all happened on this porch.

Page 71
The Maury   We waited until the light was just right and the river was as still as a mirror. Bruce captured this image that everyone sees, and has seen for over 100 years.

Page 72-73
Rail's-Eye View   Standing side-by-side, we took photos here because the light was just perfect—that broken golden light, right at sunset. Bruce made this image of the tracks because you can't think of Buena Vista without the historic contribution of the railroad.

Page 74
The Building Supply   We chose this image that Bruce shot because of the great texture. It's almost patriotic in worn red, white, and blue. We walk or drive past this building daily and love the little details.

Page 75
Autumn   Another backyard sunset image made by Jenny of Maples in the fall—it's literally homey and comforting, white picket fence and all.

Page 77
R.E. Lee Memorial Episcopal   When snow starts to fall, Bruce gets ready to go outside, looking for pictures. This image of the church's side door has a timeless quality.

Page 78-79
Lexington Presbyterian   The steeple returned in 2002 after a catastrophic fire in 2000 and Jenny made this holiday image to commemorate the reconstruction. Jenny also made an image of the burning steeple that was featured on the cover of Preservation Magazine.

Page 80-81
Jackson Hall   The door at Christmas provided Bruce with a classic holiday image, but the scene inside the hall, shot with a 16 mm lens, offers a tremendous sense of the space. You can actually see behind yourself at the top of this image.

Page 82-83
Lee Chapel   Bruce caught this twilight image on a cold winter night with a long exposure that brings up the color that's actually there but you rarely see.
Jackson Hall Window   From the outside looking in, Bruce made this image of the flags… In the lower right corner is the reflection of the American flag in front of the VMI barracks, in the lower left are the flags hanging inside the hall.

Page 84
At Rest   This is an image that Jenny planned and really wanted to make. She shot the recumbent sculpture of General Lee with a 16 mm lens to include the entire atmosphere that surrounds him.

Page 85
Moon over Lexington   This exceptionally cold winter image was taken by a gloveless Bruce from our front yard. One of the things about living here in Rockbridge: you become aware of the elements you just don't see in the big city—sky, sunsets, stars. On a clear night we can see the Milky Way from our yard.

Page 86
Flag at the Cemetery   Bruce was on his way to do the picture on page 87 when he saw the bright red against the colorless winter stones. It's really a routine Lexington sight… honoring the ancestors.

Page 87
Stonewall in the Snow   There is something about snow in graveyards—the acute hard lines, the way the black path reaches out to you. You see the world around you with fresh eyes in the snow.

Page 88
Old Chessie Trestle   While fishing with his brother-in-law, Bob, on the South River, Bruce saw this image and returned the next morning to make the shot. The power lines, normally something to be avoided, help the graphic balance of the scene. Notice the morning fog in the background, slowly burning off in the sunshine.

Page 89
The Mill Wheel   Jenny wanted a mill wheel shot and found the detail she was looking for at Wade's Mill in Raphine. There are so many wheels around Rockbridge, we could have filled the book just with mill wheels. This image is really about the interplay of shapes. Jenny often picks a detail over a photo of the whole object.

Page 90
Heirloom Garden   The Herb Farm is a popular stopping place in northern Rockbridge. Jenny saw the fence first, then the cloches. The subtle hues and reflections drew her to make this photograph… and it's her favorite image in the book—reminiscent of Mr. MacGregor's Garden, minus the rabbits.

Page 91
Stars and Bars   Still in the Raphine area, Jenny made this drive-by shot, attracted to the textures of the old wood and metal. The broken window at the top gives it context and scale.

Page 92-93
Reflecting the Bridge   Cedar Creek nearly went dry in the summer of 1999. Bruce took the opportunity to capture a new way to look at this international icon. You can't get the rocks or this crisp, mirror reflection when the water is up.

Page 94
The Traditional View   This is the view most people remember of the Natural Bridge. The emphasis for Bruce in making this picture is on the lines and color of the empty benches.

Page 95
Folded Rock   Jenny captured the distinctive formations in the Natural Bridge Cavern. This image was a slow, hand-held shot, with available light. We never stop being astonished by the things that nature does.

Page 96
Blue Ridge Barn   This image was taken by Bruce in the Collierstown area while on a family car ride. It's just a nice evening photo and typical of the area farms nestled in the valley.

Page 97
The Old Trees   This image captured by Bruce is all about the color of the pale sky and the gnarled graphic of the trees… They're Rockbridge trees and they've been there a long time watching history march past.

Page 98-99
Cold Creek   This is one of the first images taken and selected for our book. The subtle colors of blue and grey in the water amplify the chilled feelings Bruce recalls when making this image. The twisted snarl of the foreground and the stillness of the barn gives this Kerrs Creek landscape a sense of place.

Page 100
Barbed Wire   This image was a surprise and Bruce doesn't recall when or where it was taken, but it proves that he can enjoy patterns too. Two different brands of barbed wire, perhaps waiting to become a fence like the one on the facing page.

Page 101
The Fence   Jenny made this image in the Mt. Vista area. It is just so typical of the Rockbridge pastoral scenery.

Page 103
Highland View   Bruce made this image while Jenny was shooting "The Fence." We can hop out of the car, look in different directions and see so many different scenes at the same place.

Page 105
Brick Leaves   Bruce made this photograph of the autumn foliage scattered on our signature brick walks—it just screams Lexington. We've heard many conflicting legends about how the bricks came to be here.

Page 107
Chavis House   Bruce just loves the mirror symmetry of this image made on Lee Street. You see this black and white in the cold light of day.

Page 110-111
Southern Gothic   This image Jenny made—at the Oxford Church near South Buffalo Creek—has all the elements… and it clearly says *The End*.

The boundaries which divide Life from Death are at best shadowy and vague.

Edgar Allan Poe